So It Is With Us

the 12 steps as a tool for Christian spiritual formation

David Drake Ray

INTRODUCTION

*Why should we use the 12 steps as a tool for
Christian spiritual formation?*

I felt apprehensive listening to a group of non-Christians talk to me about God—who God is, what He could do for me, how He required me to live my life, and what He had done for them. After all, I considered myself an experienced Christian. I was the one with a B.A. in Religious Studies, an M.A. in Christian Apologetics, the son of an evangelical pastor, and a former pastor myself. How could these people teach me to live according to God's design? Some of them openly confessed that they didn't even know who God is! What could they give me in the way of a solution to the spiritual dilemma I found myself in, a dilemma which threatened my very life? Why should I listen to them and actually consider implementing their suggestions?

To begin with, I was broken and needed help. My solutions did not work. I was spiritually bankrupt and knew it. I was the worst kind of person: I knew all about God; I could quote readily from Scripture and debate the orthodoxy of this or that position; I could teach the Bible and supplement it with history, reason, philosophy, and science. But when it came to applying it to my own life, I couldn't. I had drunk myself into alcoholism, I was separated from my wife and soon to be divorced, and I had left my legal career in shame and disrepute. I was economically shattered, emotionally empty, and physically dying.

My desperate situation made me willing to listen to people who had overcome the very struggles I was inept at solving. They lived consistent, principled lives. They were peaceful and free. I wanted what they had and was willing to go to any lengths to get it—including letting them instruct me on the path to a deeper and more effective relationship with God. They may not have had the theological training and experience I did, but they possessed the key to unlock the power of that knowledge. This is a bold statement, to be sure, but one which I feel comfortable making now that I am living in the very same consistency, peace and freedom that I once so glaringly lacked.

As hopeless as I was, I wasn't willing to sacrifice my faith in Jesus. Lest I sound too heroic, let me rephrase: at the time, I was too scared that I was going to die that I wasn't going to part with my faith, the last remnant of hope I had for forgiveness of my countless sins. I was pleased to discover that the process they introduced me to didn't conflict with my faith in Christ, for it actually supported and came from it. They spoke of getting rid of my anger, of my problem with selfishness and arrogance, of the need to confess my sins to God in the presence of another person, of righting my wrongs as far as I was able to do, and of the necessity of helping others in the same way I had been helped. They were telling me to put deeds to my faith. Of course—why hadn't I thought of that before? I had, but as a concept, rather than a concrete, guiding principle that produced real, physical action on my part. I was the example, if there ever was one, of James' admonition that "faith without works is dead." I had the faith, yet I was almost dead. It was time to act.

So I did—and I was freed. Freed to treat others with sincere love, not out of guilt or shame. Freed to worship God in spirit and truth. In my own experience I found that actively working the 12 steps brought me into a deeper and more effective relationship with God. My ideas of what a disciple of Christ should do and who I am in relationship to God, other Christians, and all people, were revolutionized. Most importantly, my life looked dramatically different: I experienced victory over alcoholism, depression, fear, confusion, purposelessness and apathy.

I felt I had finally tapped into the reality and power of Jesus' teachings, of His life and sacrifice for us. Isn't this what many of us have always hoped for?

After I recovered I soon came to believe that the step process can be used by any Christian to help him or her reconnect with God. I don't believe the steps add anything to our faith; however, through step work, we are able to contextualize and apply biblical teachings in a tangible way. We can put flesh to our beliefs.

This process isn't intended to be used only by Christians who are seeking recovery from a particular addiction or compulsive behavior. Why should this process be limited to Christians with obvious issues? The 12 steps are a powerful tool to bring anyone into a deeper, more meaningful and authentic relationship with God. Who of us, at one time or another, hasn't wanted to be closer to God, to be used by Him in a more powerful way, and to achieve victory over the sins that ensnare us? What the steps offer us as Christians is a simple set of tools to apply Christ's teaching to our lives.

Please be assured that this process will not challenge Christian orthodoxy. What it will challenge is our selfishness and the gap between our faith and our works. My hope is that many of you will experience, as I did, liberation from the apathy, confusion and uselessness that so easily cripple us and make us question God's power in our lives. My promise to you is that a rigorous application of the steps will bring you to a deeper relationship with God and His genuine, abiding peace.

There are many approaches to the 12 steps and varied adaptations. The steps have been reformatted for Christians in other books by people much more qualified and eloquent than I. I am not doing anything novel or new. My attempt here is to isolate and re-contextualize the steps, as I took them, into the Christian faith. This small pamphlet is intended to be an easy and brief practical outline to effectively work the step process. Most importantly, this pamphlet should not be read alone; it should be used as a supplement for one-on-one or small group settings. It is intended to be a spring board only, for we need to work this process with someone who has already been through it. As we work through these few pages, an experienced sponsor or small group facilitator will insert his or her own experience and story into the process. That will be infinitely more helpful and powerful than anything contained here.

You will notice that the steps are not laid out in a step-per-chapter format. I assure you that this is not a purposeful attempt to frustrate or confuse anyone. Rather, I believe there is a certain organic grouping of the steps that is lost when they are discussed in isolation from one another.

CHAPTER I

I remember standing in my new office on the 23rd floor, looking at the Pacific Ocean out of my windows. I could see Malibu to the north and Catalina Island in the distance to the south. The autumn sun was setting, casting an orange glow across west Los Angeles. I was a freshly minted entertainment attorney coming straight out of law school into a dream job for one of the major film studios. Very few attorneys, even after years of practice in L.A., are ever given the opportunity to stand where I was and I knew it. I had arrived. It was a magical moment as I starred at the new letterhead with the studio logo and my name on it. "This is really happening," I thought to myself as chills travelled down my spine. I stood there and relished the knowledge of a New England boy done good.

But it was short lived. A few moments later the only thought that consumed my mind was how long it would be before I could get my hands on a drink. The splendor of the moment was gone. In a flash my office turned from a cathedral of the American dream to a prison cell. I knew that I should have been content, yet I was deeply convicted that I wasn't. I left work that day and drank. The next day it was the same, a pattern that repeated for the next three years. Every day I woke up with the same resolve to not drink, and every day I ended up drinking. My prayers grew more earnest and desperate while my life and relationships crumbled around me.

Convinced that I needed a deeper relationship with God, and with much prodding from my family, I joined a local church, got involved in a small group and was even asked to be a member of a leadership team for Christian education. I dabbled in AA and went to a prestigious rehab. Nothing worked. My drinking got worse and the consequences got bigger. I had faith in God and believed in the resurrecting power of Jesus; before law school I had even been an assistant pastor down the street in Beverly Hills. What was wrong? Where was God? I prayed and prayed but nothing changed. I was powerless to change and my life was out of control and getting worse. My shame and guilt grew as I continually wasted countless chances given to me by my family, employer and loved ones.

I became fearful and was plagued with anxiety and doubt. I saw psychiatrists, therapists, and counselors. I tried several different medications, all of which held the promise of a cure, but nothing worked. The only constant truth I felt was the knowledge that I was a sinner. My conviction of sin was omnipresent. I clung to 1 John 1:9, "If we confess our sins, he is faithful and just and will forgive us our sins and purify us from all unrighteousness." I wrote the verse on a piece of paper and carried it in my wallet. Instead of using the verse as a call to change, however, it became a get out of jail free card that would clear my conscience temporarily.

The daily reinforcement that I could be forgiven of my sin became an enabling force instead of an efficacious force for change. Selfishly, I used the grace of God as an excuse to continue in my sin. I answered Paul's rhetorical question in Romans 6:1, "What shall we say then? Shall we go on sinning so that grace may increase?" with a resounding "Yes." But I stopped enjoying the sin; I became a slave to it. The promises of restoring my career, reconciling with my estranged wife, and saving my body from the ravages of alcohol were all unable to produce any change in me. I was powerless and I knew it.

In a strange way, I was fortunate. My sin was open and obvious. It was having devastating effects on my life and couldn't be ignored. I tried to put on a good face and pretend I was alright with my loved ones, friends and colleagues, but after a while there was no way I could get away with it. If I didn't deal with it then I would end up in jail or dead.

This isn't the case with all sin, though. Many Christians are enslaved by sin that is much more subtle, yet terminal for the soul. What motivation is there to change for the man who has an extreme case of self-righteousness and pride? Externally his life can look absolutely amazing; a beautiful home, lovely children and a sizeable savings. But inside he is filled with emptiness, anger and doubt. He is driven to succeed because without success he feels worthless, and others who are not striving to the same ends do, in fact, become worthless in his eyes. So he surrounds himself with others who think and act the same. He soon discovers that he must maintain the appearance of worthiness or else lose the friendship of those he has surrounded himself with. He has shallow and meaningless relationships, leading to more emptiness, anger and doubt, producing more striving, and so on. He can maintain the appearance that all is well, but he knows it is not. He is trapped. Moreover, he passes these traits on to his children and re-enforces them in the people he spends his time with. There aren't enough social or societal forces to push him out of this cycle, so he remains in it until death or a catastrophe thrusts him out of it. He is powerless, in and of himself, to change. And so he is doomed to look righteous and successful but remain filled with loneliness and remorse.

And then there are those who struggle with chronic hypocrisy. There is a brilliant anecdote in the book of James about hypocrisy: "Suppose a brother or sister is without clothes and daily food. If one of you says to him, 'Go, I wish you well; keep warm and well fed,' but does nothing about his physical needs, what good is it?" (James 2:14-16). How is this hypocritical? The well wisher claims to have life-changing faith in God but doesn't act on it beyond wasting a few breaths. Could it get more hypocritical? We hypocrites throw a Bible verse in your face after you've shared your doubts about the existence of God and you've spent the night weeping. We hypocrites say that we'll pray for you when you have just been diagnosed with cancer, and maybe we'll throw your name up to God in a passing prayer. "Oh... and please God, bless so and so during her fight to the death with cancer. Amen." Haven't we all done this? We hypocrites tell you we'll pray for you and really mean it. Yet when we run into you a few days later—and remember that we completely forgot to pray for you—we say something like, "Hey, how are you? I've been praying for you. How's it going?" Now we are liars, too! The insidiousness of hypocrisy is that terminal hypocrites keenly recognize it in others and become bitter toward them for the very things they themselves do; they become bigger hypocrites.

Then there are the saddest cases: those of us who have come to a point of hopelessness and apathy. We have tried our hardest to connect with God. We pray, go to Bible studies, join small groups, volunteer for local charities, join the choir or worship team, become deacons or elders, and take the latest spiritual class (like the 12 steps for Christian formation), but there is still that feeling of disconnectedness. We ask why God isn't using us in a greater capacity and why our faith is so dry. We strive and strive to earn God's favor, to please Him in the ways we know how, but still have that feeling of distance from Him. And so we change churches, hoping that this new group of people can finally help us or will see our hidden spiritual talents and use them appropriately. Or we change our ministry focus or we switch service projects. For a time we are filled with newness and hope, but it fades and we are stuck in the same rut again. Then, oh and then, we begin to question if there is any church or group of believers out there that is really doing God's will. We lose hope, get tired and fade.

For me, the most frightening aspect of these subtle sins is that we all practice them at one time or another in varying degrees; furthermore, there are acceptable levels of this behavior, especially in the church. Who of us doesn't like to be seen talking or spending time with the "righteous" and "well-to-do" people in our community of believers? And isn't it simply accepted that when I say, "I'll pray for you," what I really mean is, "Good luck with that"?

The common thread through our lives, whether our sin in obvious or subtle, is our powerlessness to change ourselves and the sins that ensnare us. No amount of effort or manipulation is effective to bring lasting peace and a perpetual experience of God's life changing power. I know—I was powerless to change myself—but why?

Our main problem is that we are disobedient and selfish; when we practice selfishness and disobedience for long enough, we become addicted to it and we lose our power to choose.

I once read a rabbi's take on how we should understand why God "hardened" Pharaoh's heart in the Exodus story. He likened Pharaoh to a heroin addict. Pharaoh had several opportunities to let the people of Israel go, but each time he chose anger and pride and refused to submit to God's command. By the time Moses warned Pharaoh that the angel of death would strike Egypt, Pharaoh had lost the power to choose to obey; he had chosen obstinacy for so long that when his son's life was threatened his heart was too hard to chose any other course of action. Similar to a drug addict or alcoholic, in the beginning he had the power to choose correctly but after repeated disobedience selfishness took root and he was powerless to choose correctly. Thus, God allowed his heart to be hardened. (Please see the Appendix entitled, "Mind/Body Disease Model.)

So it is with us. Sure, we say and do the "big things" right: we pay our bills and taxes, we show up for church on time, we're not drinkers or gluttons (or maybe we are). But what about the details? What about that gossip on the phone? What about the favoritism shown to the person who has wealth? What about the prayers for financial blessing so we can get that shiny new thing? If we look carefully at *all* of our actions, and not just what we think are the major ones, we find that we are acting, for the most part, selfishly. Our main motivations are self-preservation, self-expansion, self-esteem, and self-advancement. These are in direct contradiction to the biblical mandate to "do nothing out of selfish ambition or vain conceit." This would explain why the more we try to manipulate God and others to serve our own ends, the less satisfied we become. If God is the only one who can bring true satisfaction and change to our lives and we act in opposition to His commands, we are doomed to discontent and unhappiness.

The good news is that Jesus has paid for these things with His death and resurrection, and God has given us His Spirit to strengthen us to change. But knowledge of this and confession of it, in and of itself, is ineffective to transform us. John writes, "We know that we have come to know him if we obey his commands. The man who says, 'I know him,' but does not do what he commands is a liar, *and the truth is not in him*" 1 John 2:3, 4. We are living a lie and deceiving ourselves. This is akin to insanity. We have a perception of ourselves and of reality that is untrue.

We must honestly look at our actions and our beliefs— all of them. Have my solemn efforts to get what I want from God failed? Am I lacking true contentment and purpose? Have all of my human attempts at self-satisfaction fallen short? Has my power to change and manage my life proved power-less? Most importantly, has my heart become hardened to God and selflessly obeying Him? Admitting this is in our own lives is the first step. Keep in mind, we don't need to admit that we are a horrible people or that we have a chronic problem with a deep dark secret (although we may come to think that both are true). We only need to come to a place where we can admit that we are powerless to bring ourselves peace and that when we try to manipulate the people and circumstances around us to make ourselves look or feel better, the results are short lived.

CHAPTER 2

I would like to share an excerpt from my journal, written during a very painful and dark period of my life when I found myself alone and contemplating the meaninglessness of life. I believe it will be helpful to us in taking the next step in this process.

I heard once that someone commented that life was "short, brutish and hard." Then what is the point of living it? And why do we have such an insistence on squeezing everything we can out of such a thing? The harder we try the shorter, more brutish and harder it gets. There seems to be built within us this insane desire to pursue, to work, to strive, to hope. Why? Have we not learned? Are those fleeting moments of joy, peace, passion, rapture, and anticipation enough to whip us to continue to get them again when ninety-nine percent of our lives is anything but? Or perhaps it is just me. This evening I found myself at a church service and the pastor was preaching on 1 Peter. He discussed the themes of suffering and hope. Odd bedfellows. Peter admonished his readers that suffering could best be understood as a purifying force, one that tests, strengthens and solidifies our belief and reliance on God and teaches us obedience. Peter wrote that suffering can be endured because we always have the hope of eternal, blissful life with God after we die.

Which leads me back to my question. If our hope is death then why, why do we live? ...What are the thoughts and reflections that have led me here? Perhaps loneliness has thrust me to consider more seriously the metaphysical, the ultimate, the eternal, the present, anything that may take me out of the current state of depression. But it doesn't work. It only makes me more empty, more low. Nor does talking with people help, it has the opposite outcome that I would hope. The pain I currently feel, as selfish and petty as it is, is most certainly real and is most certainly debilitating. I have felt pain before, real pain. I've felt physical, emotional, and spiritual pain...So I feel capable to at least identify the pain I have now. And yes, it is most certainly pain of a severe nature. The problem is that pain can be tolerated if there is hope that it will end. I have had hope in the past and that hope, whatever it may have looked like in the particular situation, allowed me to endure the pain. But now, tonight, there is no hope and therefore the pain becomes unbearable for that reason and that reason alone.

Obviously I wrote this in a state of desperation and pain. I had come to a point where I knew I couldn't manage my life through my own power. But where was God? I knew if He would only show me the light at the end of the tunnel I would be okay. But I couldn't see it; everything was dark. Without hope, life becomes futile, because hope is the very thing that brings us through pain and emptiness—without it we are lost and alone. We, as humans, have the unique capacity to remain in pain and suffering if there is good reason for it, if we know that it will end and better things will come out of it. Who of us hasn't sat resolutely while a dentist injects a needle into our mouths to numb us from greater pain? We endure that painful pinching feeling because we know that it will save us from feeling the drill!

The night I wrote that journal entry, I couldn't see how the pain was going to end. It was too deep, too real. I didn't know why God was not answering my prayers—didn't He love me? I so badly wanted to discount Peter's words that "the God of all grace, who called you to his eternal glory in Christ, after you have suffered a little while, will himself restore you and make you strong, firm and steadfast" (I Peter 5:10). It made me angry. I felt I was being toyed with, that God was intentionally allowing my spirit to be crushed for no good reason.

But consider Peter and what he wrote. His words were born from personal experience. From all accounts, Peter loved Jesus. He had left his home and career to follow Jesus and become a leader of the disciples. But on the night before Jesus' crucifixion, to save himself from being arrested, Peter denied three times that he even knew who Jesus was. In the book of Luke, we are even told that Jesus was standing there watching Peter's denial, looking straight at him! The following days must have been some of the loneliest and darkest any man on earth has ever endured. Jesus was dead. Peter had lost hope. What was he going to do? How could he go home and explain his denial to his wife, his neighbors, and his friends? He had lost three years of his life following a now-executed teacher and prophet. Would he be arrested and killed himself? No hope was left. Soon thereafter the resurrected Christ appeared to Peter and forgave and restored him.

Peter lived through the pain and he knew what he was talking about, for he had experienced the darkness, too. Knowing this, Peter's words, "after you have suffered a little while, [He] will *himself* restore you," carry great weight. The resurrected Christ appeared to Peter, forgiving and restoring him. These were deeply personal words. He wasn't simply pontificating or writing in platitudes. He trusted that because God had brought hope to him, He would bring hope to others as well.

Coming to believe that God can bring sanity to our lives—that is, bring our actions in line with our beliefs—may seem easy. But for me, it most certainly wasn't. I had desperately asked God to bring change to my life and I knew the change I asked for was according to His will for me. I wanted victory over sin—isn't this the central message of the scriptures? I prayed and prayed, but no victory came; in fact, my sin grew larger and so did my despair. Mentally, I felt forced into the position that either 1) God didn't exist or 2) God had left me. I can tell you, with everything that is within me, entertaining those thoughts brings overwhelming darkness. I felt betrayed, lonely and angry. The pain was unbearable and there was no hope that I could see. There is hope, however, for victory and peace. God is real, and He didn't leave me. When I came to the end of myself, I was closer to experiencing God's power than I had ever been before.

I remember sitting in detox, coming off alcohol for the last time. I had been served divorce papers and fired from my job. The shame and humiliation were unbearable. My small group counselor was taking a few of us through a meditation exercise. Tears ran down my face as I thought of my ex-wife, of the pain and torment I had caused her, and of the hopelessness of my future. My life, as I knew it, was over and I was to blame. Where was I to go from here? Had I been doomed to an early grave it would have seemed a relief, but a few weeks later I was introduced to people who had been in the same situation and recovered. If God had healed them, would He do it for me? Was there hope after all?

There is hope that God can restore us and bring us into a new and more useful life. God doesn't change; if He has done it for me and others, He can certainly do it for you. At the time, I didn't know the how or why, but I knew that my efforts to fix my life had failed. That is exactly where God allows us to get, though, because that is when we allow His power to work in us. When we have nothing left we are willing to accept His strength because we have nowhere else to go. The point of suffering and pain is to compel us to acknowledge our absolute reliance on God. This is why God allows it. Why would we ever turn to Him if we didn't think we needed His help? God permits us to fail so that He can show His victory.

The victory can be yours, too. Rationally we are left with no other alternative. If God restored Peter after he denied Christ, if God healed me of alcoholism even though my own selfishness and fear caused it, then we must admit that He can restore you, as well. If He can't, then He isn't God.

Notice I'm not asking you to admit that God *will* restore and bring new meaning to your life. That is not yet the point. The second step in the process is believing that God *can* bring us to a point where our faith and actions match, that He *can* restore us and bring peace to our lives. And you can know that He has done it for me because I have lived it. People can choose to ignore words but they cannot ignore experiences. We can rely on the reality of the lives that have been brought from darkness into light.

Hope. This is what the second step brings. If God has worked miraculously in the lives of others then He can work miraculously in anyone's life. He can, so there is hope. And if there is hope then the frustration, the pain, the apathy, the emptiness, the loneliness, and the desperation can be endured. Right now, at this very moment, God is perfecting your faith, not destroying it. God allowed me to experience doubt and pain so that I had nowhere to turn but to Him.

It was a few months before I finally got sober; I was nearing the end of my alcoholic insanity. I remember that October: my ex-wife had, understandably, left our home in Los Angeles and I was drinking very heavily every day. Whiskey and coke—I can still feel its horrible, stinging smell. I was constantly watching a movie based on Johnny Cash's life. In heavy rotation on one of the movie channels, it always seemed to be on when I came home from work, a fresh bottle of whiskey in my briefcase and loneliness awaiting me in an empty home. I would have a few strong drinks and watch the movie as I got ready to go out to a bar. What misery.

Part of me knew I wasn't going to last. I knew, somewhere within me, something had to give but I didn't know what. I had no plans for the future because I wasn't sure there was one. But there was always that damn movie. Within it there was a longing that some force, some event, some something could happen and thrust me out of that existence. I identified with Johnny Cash's plight: a wife who hated him, drug and alcohol addiction, and the longing for a love that would accept him and help him become something else. The alcohol fueled the delusion that I, like Johnny Cash, was a rock star of sorts. An entertainment attorney who flashed money and talked a big game, I *was* a star in the circles I chose to run in. L.A. is a funny town like that—you can feed your ego and prop up your pathetic life if you have the right business card.

But I have a different reaction to the movie now. It doesn't hold the power it once did for me, for it is someone else's story, not mine. My hope is now from my own journey. The love that helped me become someone else was

God, not a woman. And my "event" was a difficult gift that was soon to be given. What a time that was. I really thought I was at the end of my life; little did I know that it was just about to start. It may be the same for many of you. There is hope that God can bring a fuller and more meaningful life, but you must believe that He can. You must come to accept that God can do for you what He has done for me and so many others.

If you have come to believe this, there is a decision to make: you must decide what to do with this hope. If I trust that God can change me, I need to act in reliance on it.

The greatest mistake I have made in my life, so far, is believing that God had to work within the parameters of my expectations. When I was praying for change and victory, I was really praying for God to restore my marriage and my career. I wanted Him to make everything better. I wanted to be free of my vices but everything else needed to look the same. The same people, the same office, the same home, the same everything save the emptiness and addiction. But God had different things in mind. He wanted my life *and* my expectations.

If we only allow God to work and move in the way we want Him to, are we really allowing Him to be God? When Jesus called Peter, what would it have looked like if Peter told Him, "Oh, yes, I will follow you, but you'll need to teach and heal people only in my town and only after I get home from work. You know, I need to make a living and I've worked hard to get where I am. Other than that, I'm with you all the way." It sounds odd but when we're honest, this is often how we treat God.

Here's the rub, if you will. God will bring change to our lives but on His terms, not ours. If we want to experience

His full life-changing power, we must be willing to allow Him full access. Can you imagine going to a doctor to have a brain tumor removed and saying, "I know you need access to my head but I really don't want any visible scars, so you'll have to come up through my foot. Oh, and I don't like sharp objects so you'll be understanding and not use a scalpel. One more thing: hospitals really make me nervous, so if you could perform the procedure in my living room, that would be most comfortable for me." Ridiculous. But it is equally absurd when I ask God to change and use me, yet I dictate to Him how He needs to change me, when He needs to do it, where He should use me and what should remain untouched. We place our care and our lives in the hands of physicians and do as we're told because they know best, not us. Should we not place our lives in the hands of the Great Physician with equal confidence?

If there is hope that God can change me I must trust everything I have and am with Him to do as He sees fit. If I don't do this, I am saying is that I know better than He does, that I don't really want everything He wants, and I only want His power under certain circumstances. But if God can't have all of you, does He have any of you? Either we trust Him or we don't. Either we give Him our lives or we keep them for ourselves. Ultimately, we are asking to use His power selfishly and haphazardly. God doesn't allow us to use His power that way. Because we are human, we would destroy ourselves and everyone around us.

We need to make a decision to turn all of our life, all of our expectations, and all of our desires over to the care of God. When I took this step I had nothing left. God removed all of the earthly trappings I had clung to. I was given the precious and costly gift of desperation. I expect that this will not be the case with many of you; however, there may be a lot to give over to God: your loves, your possessions, and your dreams.

But God can be trusted with these things. He is not out to harm us; trust me, if He wanted to do that He already would have, in the most cruel and calculated ways. God made us to live lives of purpose and joy, the very traits of a life that is in unity with God. The life of the person who has fully yielded to the Spirit of God within them has "love, joy, peace, patience, kindness, goodness, faithfulness, gentleness and self-control" (Gal. 5:22b). Isn't this what we are all searching for anyway? The problem is that we think we can get these things ourselves if we try hard enough or if we work long enough. That is why we refuse to hand our lives over to God, because we are afraid He will to take away the things we think will eventually bring us love, joy and peace. Nothing is farther from the truth. If all the possessions and relationships and aspirations we refuse to give over to the care of God were going to bring these things to us, they already would have done so. No one would be reading this.

I am not saying that we need to sell all of our possessions, leave our loved ones, and sport a wool robe. No (although it may be an interesting and entertaining experiment). What I am suggesting is that we give God the authority to do with them as He would desire, that we give our will and our life over to the *care* of God. Although God is the ultimate creator and owner of everything, He has given us the power to choose whether to do this or not. It is a tremendous power. With it, humanity has perpetrated incalculable evil and pain on itself. We have chosen war over peace, hate over love, punishment over mercy, ignorance over understanding; but there have also been those who have chosen to give control of their lives to God, and they are shining stars who bring hope and light. The prime example of this is Jesus Himself.

The night before He was executed, Jesus stood at a turning point. He could have bailed. His life could have continued. He could have gone to the temple that night and taken control of the country and, eventually, the world. He could have set up for Himself an earthly empire never to be rivaled—an empire with extreme power and prosperity. We never really stop to consider that. We all know the story of Jesus' temptation by Satan in the wilderness, but at the time He was battling hunger rather than torturous execution. Chances are that during His life Jesus saw people hanging on crosses. He knew what it looked like. I imagine that He may have paused once or twice during His prior visits to Jerusalem and peered at the men hanging there, tortured and ridiculed. When we think of this we begin, and I mean *only* begin, to understand why He would have prayed, "Father, if you are willing, take this cup from me."

God understands. He knows our fear of relinquishing control to Him. What will it mean? What will my life look like? What if I don't like what God has in store for me? Most likely, though, you are not concerned that God will require you to be nailed on a cross tomorrow. Our concerns are relatively petty and selfish. We are more concerned with maintaining the creature comforts we have become accustomed to. What will God do with my down time? My weekends? Will He really require me to love the people I hate? Will I have to understand and tolerate people whom I disagree with politically and socially? Do I have to stop gossiping and being the center of attention? Does He really expect me to turn the other cheek, and let my actions speak instead of my words? Yes, and more. He wants to bring us to a place where we can say to Him, "Not my will, but yours be done."

How are we to get to this point? Jesus was able to submit His will and life to God because He knew that the result would be peace and joy: "for the joy set before Him [He] endured the cross" (Heb. 12:2). And that is our hope: that God will finally bring joy and peace if we submit our lives to Him. Our human attempts at creating lasting peace and joy have failed. We have all tried at times (and perhaps over long periods of time) to get what we can out of this life for ourselves. We keep trying to make ourselves happy through love, sex, money, pride, control, volunteering, church membership, or adherence to the right ideology. Underlying these is a selfish motive to get what we can out of life; we put ourselves first but always find that it's not enough. So, we try to get more of "it" thinking that more of "it" will finally do what less of "it" couldn't. Insane.

Consider this: God made the universe and He made the rules. He tells us to live our lives unselfishly, considering others first, so that we will do His will and find peace. Yet we act selfishly, thinking that if we can get what we want out of our lives then we'll finally find the peace and purpose that has been eluding us. We think that if we could only have that house or a better job, everything would be alright. Or if such and such happened everything else would be fine. So we strive and plot and scheme *and pray* to get to that magical place, a fairy land where all is well and we want for nothing. If you ever find that place, you will be the only inhabitant because no one lives there. It is a fantasy—that place does not exist in the universe God created. Augustine's words are as true today as they were centuries ago: "Restless are our hearts until they find rest in Thee." Our efforts to find rest, peace and purpose are futile if they are selfish. Only by living our lives by God's design can we find the rest only He can provide.

Listen to James. "You lust and do not have; so you commit murder. You are envious and cannot obtain; so you fight and quarrel. You do not have because you do not ask. You ask and do not receive, because you ask with wrong motives, so that you may spend it on your pleasures."

What are we to do? We must draw near to God and He will draw near to us. We must submit our lives to God and He will give life to us. Once we do this we'll find that He will provide everything we need. Our Father will take care of our material and spiritual needs if we rely on Him to do so. Jesus tells us, "Do not seek what you will eat and what you will drink, and do not keep worrying. For all these things the nations of the world eagerly seek; but your Father knows that you need these things. But seek His kingdom, and these things will be added to you."

There is a whole new existence to be had! God promises a life without crippling anxiety, a life full of purpose and contentment, a life with deep communion and love, a life without confusion, a life with fulfillment. The striving can cease and the burden be lifted. We no longer have to make decisions based on what others think; we now care about what God thinks. Once guilt and shame are cleared away, we begin to experience a deep conviction that God can and does work through us in ways we can't imagine. Many of us experience it now. It is amazing what God can do with our lives if we only allow Him to do it. If God has the power to create the universe, He can re-create our lives—but we must choose to let Him.

When you are ready to take this step, to finally give everything to God, it is best to do it in community with others who have taken it or who covenant to take it with you. It is a serious and solemn act and, although it is a personal decision, our lives are built and lived with others. We need to publically and communally hand ourselves over to the care of God. There is no set way to do it, but we have developed a little tradition that seems to work. When we gather with people who are taking this step we kneel in a circle, bow our heads, hold hands and say a prayer together. The prayer is simple and similar to this: God, I now give myself, all of my life and expectations, over to You to do with as You desire. I ask You to remove selfishness and disobedience from me. Please free me from slavery to myself, so that I can do Your will. May Your power be demonstrated in my life so that others will see it and believe, and may I do Your will always. Amen.

Although God can do as He wishes experience shows that this is just the beginning of our part of the work. Talk is cheap and so are prayers unless they are followed by action. Remember, when Jesus prayed "not my will but Yours be done" He didn't run and hide, He stayed and got to the work His Father had for Him. So it must be with us.

CHAPTER 3

God doesn't change. Change is a product of time, and God does not exist in time. He created time, a construct of light and gravity, but he is not bound by it. God simply is. If God cannot change, that means His character and attributes don't change. God's love and mercy, His standards, and all of who God is never changes. God loves you the same today as He did ten years ago and will love you the same ten years from now. His law never changes and, thankfully, neither does His grace.

We do change. Our bodies change: we grow, then shrink and die. Our attitudes and personalities change too. We are affected by our experiences, our choices, and the people whom we interact with. We are bound by time—there is no way to escape it. Change, then, is constant for us, but it doesn't even exist for God. Can you imagine if He did change, though? Perhaps an easy way to imagine the consequences of God changing is to picture what would happen if gravity changed. Even the slightest temporary change in gravity would cause every skyscraper to be lifted up and then smashed to the ground. Our planet could suddenly escape the sun's grasp and spin off into a cold, dark oblivion. The consequences of a change in gravity would be catastrophic. Without even thinking about it, we believe that the laws of physics are constant and we build our lives and civilizations assuming it. How much more so should it be with God? We rely on God remaining constant. We assume that He won't suddenly change the rules of the game, that Jesus' death and resurrection redeem us, and that He has an ultimate plan for humanity.

When we come to a point of spiritual dryness, however, our first reaction is to point not to ourselves but to God, as if He has changed His behavior and removed Himself from us. We begin to question who He is—perhaps we didn't really know the "true" nature of God. Finally we wonder if God exists at all. It was that way with me. I had spent years in professional study of who God is, how to demonstrate His existence, and how He revealed Himself to mankind. I was convinced; I believed! But when I became deeply entrenched in sin and selfishness and began to feel the consequence in my life, I questioned the nature and existence of God. How could He let this happen to me? How could an all-powerful and loving God not answer my prayer or give me what I needed to survive? I felt that if He did exist, He had changed toward me and left my life. As I mentioned before, during my darkest moments, when my prayers were most earnest, I experienced the greatest silence from Him—or so I thought.

How foolish I was. Any outside observer could easily point out that it wasn't God who changed, it was I. The choices I made and the liberties I took clouded my vision and I was blocked from His light and truth. When I was introduced to a program of recovery I was told that I needed to make a fearless and thorough inventory of myself, not of God. I needed to clear away the things that were blocking me from Him. This is the next step in the process and I encourage you to embrace it. Without fearlessly and thoroughly working this step, we will not experience even a fraction of what this process has to offer.

Step four requires us to make a searching moral inventory of ourselves—but what do we mean by "moral?" As a Christian I am quite accustomed to asking forgiveness for my sins. At first blush, taking a moral inventory of myself may look like writing down all of the bad things I have done and taking stock of them, but that is not what we do this time. God's law is a law of love. Jesus' command to us is simple: love one another as He has loved us. If our greatest moral act is love, then our greatest moral failure is hate.

The more resentment we have the less we are capable of love. Throughout our lives we encounter people, places and situations that cause us to get angry and resentful. Over time we accumulate resentment, until it changes us and blocks us from God. Anger and resentment build up around our spiritual eyes until we cannot see clearly any longer. God, then, begins to look different, as though He has changed. John tells us, "Whoever hates his brother is in the darkness and walks around in the darkness; he does not know where he is going, because the darkness has blinded him." This is how we block ourselves from God's power: by holding on to anger. And so hate, anger and resentment (if they are any different) are the primary ways we block ourselves from Him. Even worse, we become slaves to resentment instead of servants of love. Our life becomes controlled by our emotions and the people and things that we hate. It's strange that way—the more we hate something or someone, the more we actually become controlled by them. God's love brings peace and freedom, while hate brings bondage and turmoil. And so we must get rid of the resentment that has built up within us, but how?

It is impossible for us to wish or will away resentment. Have you ever tried? I have, and it doesn't work. Feelings are feelings; in fact, we have no ability to merely "will away" any feeling or emotion. That is what makes feelings and emotions qualitatively different from thoughts and actions; we have very little, if any, mental control over them. But these feelings are blocking us from God and we must get rid of them if we are to be of service to Him and to experience the fullness of His power in our lives.

Here's what we do: we take physical action. We're not going to ignore the fact that we can't wish away these feelings of resentment—we are going to address them. We make a list of all the people, events, institutions and principles that we resent. We write them out on paper in a column. As we do this, we ask God to show us those things that are blocking us from loving Him and our neighbors. Remember, this is a fearless and thorough inventory. Don't leave off names because you feel that you don't have the right to be angry or resentful in any particular instance. We have all tried that before and it doesn't work. In this first column of our inventory we do not attempt to rationalize our anger; we simply admit it, honestly. To the extent that we can be honest about these feelings will we be freed from them. Our candor in completing this first column exhaustively is key to the success of this process.

When I made this list, one of the names on it was God. This frightened me. What right did I have to be angry at God? I am a sinful, selfish man and my life demonstrated it. He had given me chance after chance and I blew them all. What would He do to me if I admitted, on paper no less, that I was angry at Him? But if I was honest with myself, I knew that I harbored resentment toward Him. I was told that thoroughness and honesty were the necessary components to complete the process, so I had to be honest about it—my life depended on it. I urge you to be honest and fearless as you do this. Freedom and peace await you.

When we are satisfied that we have completed this list thoroughly and honestly we move on to the second column of our inventory. Here we list why we hold resentments against each person, event, institution or principle. Sometimes there will be several items for each, sometimes only one. Practically, it is easier to number the first column and begin the second column on a new piece of paper or notebook (this provides the needed space). As a reminder, it is wise to write this prayer at the top of each new page: "God, show me those things that are blocking me from loving You and my neighbors." This prayer should become constant during this process.

During work on our second column we must evaluate our lives and touch some deep pain. It is a gut wrenching process to relive some of these moments and experiences. You may find that your anger toward these people or things actually increases as you remember and document it. This will pass; however, it is quite uncomfortable when you're in the midst of it, so it is prudent to be purposeful about completing it. It is not advisable to sit in the second column of your inventory too long. Once we have completed this column, we review it prayerfully and ask ourselves if anything has been omitted. You should ask your sponsor to review it before you move on. If you are convinced you have completed it, then you can move on to the third column.

At this point in our inventory we look back at our resentments and ask why we became angry. Humans are inherently selfish and ego driven. Our anger is usually born from our pride being hurt, our security being threatened or our way of life being endangered. So we ask ourselves specifically why we became resentful. Did it affect our pride and ambition, our self esteem, our financial security or our personal relationships, or our sexual relationship? We list these next to each resentment. Sometimes all of these will be affected by a resentment, sometimes only one. Remember, be honest.

For example, I may harbor resentment against John for receiving a promotion instead of me and for not attending my birthday party. My first three columns would look like this:

(name)	(resentment)	(Affects my)
John	A. For getting a promotion instead of me	P/A, SE, $, P/SR
	B. For not attending my birthday party	P/A, SE, P/SR

Notice I'm not resentful at John "for being a jerk." Well, maybe I am, but that's not specific enough for the fourth step. The more precise we are the more precisely we can address our hate. Generalizations are ineffective when it comes to this process. It is helpful to continually ask yourself "why" while you are completing the first three columns. If my first thought is that I'm mad at John for being a jerk, then I need to ask myself why. Once I get to specific instances I am able to progress to the next column and ask why I became angry.

After we complete the first three columns, we should have a detailed, tangible list of our resentments. Tragically, this is as far as many of us will ever go. You have in your hand an inventory of the dirt that has built up around your heart that is blocking you from God's love and power. Most people spend their lives with this layer of anger around their soul; our world is a reflection of that fact. It is time to circumcise our hearts.

In the fourth column we turn our gaze intently on ourselves. We have focused on the wrongs others have done to us for too long; they are keeping us from God and so we must put them aside. We may have been innocent victims of horrible acts or we may be culpable accomplices in our own hatred. It makes no difference—either way the anger still exists. In the fourth column we stop considering the acts of others and ask where we have been selfish, self-seeking, dishonest and frightened. We ask these four questions for each and every resentment we have listed. As we work through this column we begin to understand why anger blocks us from God; holding on to anger is unjustified. As Paul states in Romans, "...all have sinned and fall short of the glory of God." Every one of us falls into the "all" category; therefore, none of us are justified to *hold on to* resentment. Anger is born from a sense of entitlement: I am entitled to be treated a certain way, I am entitled to have certain things, I am entitled to do what I want, I am entitled to be free of pain. According to the Bible, we are entitled only to death. This should not lead to a false sense of worthlessness, not at all. One of the paradoxes of the Christian faith is that each human has eternal and immortal value, yet, because of our sin, each of us deserves to be destroyed. The fourth column isn't about making us feel worthless; it's about making us see our sinfulness. So we ask why we have been selfish for getting angry or for holding onto the anger. How am I self-seeking in this resentment? How has the image I want to portray to others been tarnished? Where am I dishonest about keeping this anger—am I being a hypocrite or were my reasons for getting angry spurious? Finally, where is the fear—does this anger make me scared or was this resentment born from fear?

Let's revisit our earlier example. My first resentment against John was that he was promoted over me. Where have I been selfish? I want to have the extra money and power; I don't care if he may need or deserve it more than I do. Self-seeking? I want to be seen as a better employee than John, more deserving of a promotion than he is. Dishonest? John actually deserves the promotion more than I do: he works harder and has been at the company longer than I have. Frightened? I'm afraid that I'll be stuck at this same job for the rest of my life, I won't be able to provide for my family, and I'll be seen as a failure.

This is a new way of thinking about and working with our anger, so it may be difficult at first. It is highly suggested that you allow your sponsor to help you along in the early stages of the fourth column until you feel you have the hang of it. Someone who has gone through this process and who writes inventory as a way of life can quickly guide you until you develop your own rhythm. But it is essential to develop a pace, for we must get through the fourth column. There isn't time to waste; the longer we tarry in doing this the more difficult it becomes to complete.

Once you have completed your resentment inventory you are ready to move on to the second phase of the fourth step: fear inventory. Fear is powerful and destructive. It may be the most powerful of human emotions. Nations use fear to manipulate, wage war and control populations. Corporations use fear to sell drugs and products that promise relief and security. Fear is a multi-billion dollar industry. For individuals, fear makes us irrational or paralyzed. Most importantly, for purposes of completing this process, fear blocks us from God. Remember, our greatest command from God is to love Him and one another. But if we are full of fear, then we can't love the way God asks us to. John writes, "There is no fear in love. But perfect love drives out fear, because fear has to do with punishment. The one who fears is not made perfect in love" (1 John 4:18).

Some astute theologians may point out that the Bible instructs us to fear: the fear of the Lord is the beginning of wisdom, work out your salvation with fear and trembling, fear Him who has the power to throw you into hell, etc. The fear that Bible instructs us to have, I believe, can be interpreted as an extraordinary respect and appreciation of who we are in relation to God and of His grace and mercy toward us. But even this fear is manipulated and twisted until legalism emerges. An appropriate understanding of the fear of God encourages us to love, while legalism gives birth to judgment and hate. The Bible tells us to fear God and nothing else, but how can we truly love God if we are horrified of Him? I think Jesus' parable of the ten minas settles the issue far greater than I ever could.

Just like anger and resentment, fear is an emotion that we must take physical action to control; thus we list our fears, just like we did our resentments. At the top of the page, write our prayer again; ask God for help, and rely on His guidance through this. Remember our third step: we have handed our wills and lives over to Him.

When we have completed listing all of our fears we address them one by one. On a new piece of paper we write a fear and then ask, "Why am I afraid of this?" When we write our answer, we ask why again. "Why am I afraid of the answer I gave?" Then we ask why again to the next answer; this continues until we reach the root fear. Most of the fears we list initially are like the fruit of a tree: these fears are simply the result of a much deeper fear. After we have completed our fear tree we are fully informed of the complexity and root of our fear.

To illustrate, let's take the fear of flying as an example:

Fear: I'm afraid of flying.

Why? Because I'm afraid of something catastrophic happening and falling from the sky.

Why? Because I hate the feeling of being trapped without being able to get out.

Why? Because I'm afraid of not having complete control.

Why? Because I don't trust God and I don't want to die that way.

Once we have gotten to the base we can turn to our part in the fear and begin to allow God to remove it.

Prior to taking the 12 steps, my life was a constant attempt to manage my fear through medication, self-knowledge, reason, alcohol, distraction, selfishness and sin. The more I tried to manage my fear through my own power, the more unmanageable it became. No amount of willpower could remove my fear. Furthermore, I didn't care how my fear management affected others. I became brutally selfish and inconsiderate in my attempts to control my anxiety. I was afraid of flying so I would get horribly drunk prior to getting on a plane. I didn't care how it would affect the people I was travelling with or the other passengers—I just wanted the fear handled. After several successful plane flights my fear proved to be unfounded, but it became an excuse for selfish and self-destructive behavior, which I continued, regardless of the fact that air travel is statistically the safest way to get around and I had the experience to prove it.

We have to get sane about our fear: where have we been selfish in harboring this fear, how has my self-reliance failed to manage or remove it, where have I been inconsiderate to others, and how have I been dishonest in holding onto it? We ask each of these four questions (selfish, self-reliance, inconsiderate, dishonest) for each of the root fears of our fear tree.

At this point we have completed two-thirds of our fourth step. The final issue we must deal with is sex. Sex is a different beast than anger and fear because sex is ordained of God but can be used to harm and manipulate others. The purpose of sex inventory is not to eliminate our sexuality, but to redeem it. Human sexuality is a complex and controversial issue, but we can't back down from dealing with it. We do so at our peril. Our society is beginning to feel the full effects of the sexual revolution, and they aren't pretty or liberating. We need to address our sexual behavior and look at it through the law of love.

The sex inventory is not merely concerned with intercourse. In fact, very little of it is. Our sexuality and powers of sex can often be used or abused without any physical contact. Through this process we aim to remove selfishness, exploitation and dishonesty. As Christians, we have a sexual standard given to us by God; however, we tend to isolate God's directives and focus merely on whom we can have sex with and when. Jesus himself took it to a much deeper (and more disturbing) level when He said, "You have heard that it was said, 'Do not commit adultery.' But I tell you that anyone who looks at a woman [or man] lustfully has already committed adultery with her [or him] in his heart." If we are held responsible for our thoughts, how much more so are we responsible for the flirtatious relationship, the wink, the teasing, or any other use of our sexual powers? If we're going to completely give ourselves to God, all of our will and all of our life, we need to give Him our sexuality, too. When we do, we will experience true sexual liberation and freedom.

Our sex inventory will look different, because we write it horizontally instead of vertically. We ask God to show us whom we have harmed, and then write their names on paper. Next to their names we record how we have harmed them—that is, what did we specifically do to harm them? In the next column we put the names of those who may have been hurt because of our selfishness, who else was affected because of our actions (this may be the most enlightening column in sex inventory), how were we inconsiderate, and finally, what we should have done differently. For instance, let's say there is a local store that I frequent because I know there is an employee working there who likes me. I have no interest in her, but she gives me a discount on my purchase every time I go there; as a result, I shop there a lot for the discount, never intending to reciprocate any feelings. Whom have I harmed? The employee who likes me. What did I do? I went there because I knew she liked me and would give me a discount. Whom did it affect? The owners of the store (they lost money), the employee's friends (they hear about how I never reciprocate feelings), and the employee's family (they want their child/sibling to find love). How was I inconsiderate? I didn't care if the store was losing money or if the employee liked me; I only wanted a discount on my purchase. What should I have done differently? I should have gone to another store, or told the employee I appreciate the discount but insist that I pay full price. When we stop and think about our actions, they affect more people than we realize. Even seemingly innocent behavior can be harmful if we are acting selfishly.

Our sex inventory will be instructive in forming an unselfish way to express our sexuality. We may have to admit improprieties, infidelity, or even abuse. We must be fearless and honest in completing this if we are to become free and have peace with God. He already knows these things. They will not shock or surprise Him. Give yourself over to the care of our Father; He loves you and His forgiveness awaits. If we insist on holding onto our secrets, they will continue to have power over us. It is time to be rid of these things that have enslaved us.

CHAPTER 4

If you've come this far, perhaps you're willing to go a bit further.

We are at the point in the process where our faith will be challenged like it may never have been before. If you've been honest and thorough with your fourth step you probably have numerous pages of dirt on yourself. You have looked at your life and actions in a way that most people don't, and it's not always pretty. You may feel that this new perspective has been enlightening and can guide you into a new way of living. To a certain extent this is true. But as followers of Jesus who want to experience something far greater than self-realization, there is more work to do.

Knowledge of truth is just that: knowledge. In our fourth step we are given a great deal of knowledge about ourselves and who we really are. But knowledge is not power. Action is power; the Spirit of God is power; love is power. Knowledge can actually bring weakness and pain if it is not acted on or if it is used to manipulate and oppress.

Prior to my recovery I had a large amount of knowledge of God, at least from a human perspective. I was enamored by knowledge. When I was a junior in college I took a New Testament survey class that blew me away. I had never looked at the scriptures in the way the professor was teaching it.

There are several layers to the gospels that I hadn't considered. In them there are political, historical, societal and cultural influences that are rarely appreciated or discussed. I was so blown away by the depth and richness of the text that I decided to change my major to religious studies. I ate the scriptures; learning how to prove the existence of God and the truth of the Christian faith became my obsession. After graduating I went on to earn a masters degree in Christian apologetics. While in graduate school I became familiar with the finer points of the Christian faith and learned how to craft a convincing argument for its authenticity. I had the truth, the knowledge, the hunger to learn more, and the desire to proclaim it from the rooftops.

In my own private life, however, I didn't apply any of it. I was drinking abusively and making harmful, selfish decisions. I couldn't live with the cognitive dissonance—knowing the truth but not living it. And so I decided to go to law school. I needed to get myself out of the truth business and into something that would fit my actions instead of my beliefs. I was walking proof that knowledge is ineffective to bring peace with God; it was crippling me because my actions were in direct conflict with the truth.

Our faith must be acted on. What good is truth if we don't do something with it? James clearly and uncomfortably articulated this principle when he wrote, "You believe that there is one God. Good! Even the demons believe that—and shudder." Why do the demons shudder? Because they have a deeper understanding of God than any of us do, but they cannot act on it—they are eternally bound and locked in hate. We now have the opportunity to act, in love, and trust that God is about to do for us what we cannot not do for ourselves.

We must admit to God, to ourselves and to another human being the exact nature of our wrongs. This is the fifth step. We must read our inventory to another person, every detail, word for word. There is no editorializing here, no rationalizations. We lay ourselves bare at the feet of God in the presence of a witness. We are going to confess our sin and our hate.

Freedom! This is what God wants to bring us. We must be free of our hate and the sin that has blocked us from God. "Yes," you say, "but why read it? Why humiliate and subject ourselves to the scorn and ridicule of another?"   Perhaps the best way to answer this is through the story of the sinful woman and Jesus. Toward the beginning of Jesus' public life he began to get the attention of the religious leaders. He was performing miracles and teaching revolutionary truths. A certain religious leader named Simon invited Jesus to his house for dinner. This would have been a large social event. Simon was hosting the newest, most intriguing teacher and preacher his country had ever seen. Even if he didn't agree with Jesus, it would increase his influence and stature to have Jesus accept his invitation to a dinner party.

So Jesus attended and was sitting (or reclining) at the dinner table. Meanwhile, there was a woman who lived in the same town who had a sinful reputation. She may have been a prostitute or even something worse; regardless, people viewed her as bad and unworthy. When she heard that Jesus was at Simon's house she grabbed a jar of perfume and headed over. Somehow, despite her reputation, she got into the house and right behind Jesus. As she listened to them talk, she began to weep; her tears flowed so badly that she got his feet wet and wiped them with her hair. Then she poured the perfume she brought on his feet. The woman never said a word, but her point is obvious. She came to Jesus to beg forgiveness for her countless sins, and she did it in public. She admitted, in the presence of a religious leader who had probably rebuked her before, her brokenness and need for the power of God to change her. What did Jesus do? He rebuked Simon and forgave the woman!

Simon wanted to increase his public image by using God's Son for his own selfish desires. The woman, in direct opposition to this, admitted that she didn't belong in the gathering but threw herself on God's grace and mercy. Keep in mind that this was a large step of faith for her. She could have been beaten and thrown out. She didn't know what Jesus was going to do—it could have gone incredibly bad. But she knew something had to change and that this Jesus may be just the guy to help her.

So in our fifth step, we are going to move from being Simon to being the sinful woman. Our inventory has demonstrated that we are far from perfect; in fact, our sin and hate is greater than we imagined. Instead of propping up our pathetic façade of righteousness and worthiness, it's time to face our powerlessness and sin and tear down the self-seeking public image we ardently protect.

When we read our inventory aloud we are also admitting to ourselves the exact nature of our wrongs. If we don't actually verbally communicate our inventory we can change our minds about it. Are we really that bad, that selfish, that dishonest? Once we read this to God, in the presence of another human being, it is final—it is out there and, best of all, out of us.

How many times have we drafted an email or a letter and then thought twice about sending it? We may think that our words really don't reflect what we mean to say or that it would be wrongly received. We may reconsider, and decide we don't want the recipient to know our thoughts and feelings. And so we don't send it. If we don't send it, we can pretend that we never wrote it; the information contained therein will remain inside of us, never to be known by anyone else. It's like that with our inventory. When we read it, we say to ourselves that we really believe this is an accurate reflection of us because we know that there is finality about the spoken word. Once words have been spoken and received, we don't have the capability to change our minds or mentally manipulate our reality. We're going for broke and there's no turning back.

This is what the sinful woman did. Whatever her issues with Simon or the other guests at the dinner party may have been, she acted on faith that Jesus would accept her and bring something new to her life. We must do the same.

The good news is that this is a confidential matter. I'm not asking anyone to disrobe in front of his or her church, friends, or colleagues. The person who hears your fifth step should be someone who can be trusted with the strongest, most delicate confidence. For the successful completion of this process it is enough that there is only one witness; no more are needed. It is recommended that you ask someone who has taken steps as they are laid out here. They will understand what you are doing and appreciate what it is you are trying to accomplish. You should meet in a private space to avoid interruptions and maintain confidentiality. Fifth steps often take several hours. If you cannot find someone who has been through this process, then the person you ask should be made aware of the time commitment and the nature of the material. If they are uncomfortable or feel that they cannot maintain a confidence, you should find someone else. We are not airing out our dirty laundry for public consumption; we are admitting to God, ourselves, and another human being the exact nature of our wrongs.

When we have finished reading our inventory we need to meditate on what we have just completed. A usual length of meditation is about an hour. During this time we are alone; our confidant will leave the room but stay in the vicinity. We consider what we have done. Have we left anything out of our inventory? Were we completely honest and thorough? Many people are physically exhausted after they read their fifth step, and this is understandable. There is only a little more to do in this phase of the process. Prayerfully deliberate on your work. If you think of something you may have left out of your inventory, ask your confidant to come back and hear it. This is your chance to be rid of it! If you are content that your work has been thorough and honest, thank God for giving you the strength He has. Thank Him that He has given you an opportunity to be honest with Him and with another person. Enjoy the silence and peace you may be feeling or rejoice in the newness God has brought to you.

At the end of your meditation it is time to take the sixth and seventh steps, alone. These are between you and God. Are you ready to have God remove these things from you? Are you ready to allow God to take the hate, fear and manipulation from your life? Can His Spirit have full sway with you? In our third step we made a decision to turn our wills and our lives over to the care of God. Now, in our sixth step, we need to become willing to have God remove the specific things that have blocked us from Him. God has forgiven us our sins through the death and resurrection of His Son. He has justified us through the cross. God wants to sanctify us through the power of His Spirit. Are we will-ing to let Him do this?

In his letter to the Galatians, Paul is trying to correct a misunderstanding that arose in their community. Christianity blossomed from the root of Judaism, and the heart of Judaism is the law. The law required males to be circum-cised. Certain Galatian followers of Jesus thus required con-verts to Christianity to be circumcised in observance of the law. It put into sharp relief the tension between observance of the Jewish law and grace from the death and resurrection of Christ. Paul knew all about the Jewish law; he was a law-yer, an expert in the law. But he knew that because of the appearance of Jesus and the demonstration of His power in rising from the dead, the law now has a different relationship to mankind. The law is perfect for showing us how sinful we are, but it is ineffective to make us righteous because it sets up an impossible standard for us to fulfill. Therefore, by re-quiring converts to be circumcised, the Galatians are relying on the law, rather than grace, to be righteous.

Paul writes, "Mark my words! I, Paul, tell you that if you let yourselves be circumcised, Christ will be of no value to you at all. Again I declare to every man who lets himself be circumcised that he is obligated to obey the whole law. You who are trying to be justified by law have been alienated from Christ; you have fallen away from grace. But by faith we eagerly await through the Spirit the righteousness for which we hope. For in Christ Jesus neither circumcision nor uncircumcision has any value. The only thing that counts is faith expressing itself through love." (Gal. 5:2-6).

In our fifth step we have felt the pinch of our hearts be-ing circumcised. We have been made aware of our hate and sin. This is the law—we are conscious of how evil we are.

But, if we are to be free of this and live in love and peace, we must now give this to God and allow His Spirit to work in us. If we rely only on the bravery and relief we have experienced by reading our inventory, then soon we will become arrogant and judgmental, just as those who insisted on observing the law became. If we are to be true worshipers of God then we must rely on faith that God's Spirit will allow us to express our faith in love.

Are you ready to have God remove these defects and replace them with the love of His Spirit? If you are willing, you have taken the sixth step. Immediately we will take the seventh. We are humbled by our inventory and willing to have God's Spirit replace our hate with His love, so we ask Him to remove our defects of character. We pray, "God, I humbly ask that you would take away these defects of character so that I can better do Your will and that victory over these sins will show others Your love, Your power and Your truth. Give me the power and love of Your Spirit because I cannot live the life you ask without it. Thank you, God, for Your forgiveness and grace."

You have now completed step seven. No doubt you have just finished something that you never thought you would do. Prayerfully, you have opened yourself up to the power of God's Spirit in a new way. Some of us may have had a sudden and extraordinary experience during our meditation time. Others may have experienced nothing. My encounter with these particular steps was simple but profound. During my meditation I was still and silent. For several minutes I sat motionless, looking out the window of the chapel I read in. Suddenly I realized that the only sound I was hearing was the noise of passing cars. I had no other thoughts racing through my head. I was, for the first time in many years, fully present in the moment.

However, we are not seeking a feeling by doing the steps. If you haven't had a profound moment, please do not be disappointed or distressed. Part of the results of working these steps is that we become less controlled by our emotions (or lack thereof). Find peace that you have walked through the heart of the steps and have demonstrated to God a sincere desire to know Him better. Rest well, for there is more work to do.

CHAPTER 5

By this point in the process we have developed a firm grasp on how selfish our lives have been. We have made a detailed list of our selfishness and openly confessed it. Now we are ready to allow God's Spirit to have control and to guide us into active lives of love. Love is not selfish. Love that is fully alive in us will always consider the needs of others first. Jesus said that perfect love is this: that we will lay down our lives for our friends. He did. He laid down His life for His friends. His words were followed by actions. It's almost like He said to His disciples, "Perfect love is when someone is willing to die so that his friend can live. You are my friends and I am going to die for you. Watch." We are called to do the same. Our words must be followed by action. Our love needs to be perfected by actively laying down our lives for others.

I quoted James' words before that faith without works is dead. If we look carefully, we see this theme throughout the teachings of Jesus. Every time Jesus says that blessed are those who hear the truth and do what it says, He is affirming this principle. Jesus was a man of action and He is calling us to be people of action. Words are easy and we have used them too often to justify ourselves or to craft an image of who we want to be seen as in the eyes of others.

The next steps we take will give us an opportunity to demonstrate, with action, the love and humility God has given us. In love we are going to go out and begin to right the wrongs we have done to others. If you are anything like me, you have said the words "sorry" or "will you forgive me?" too many times. In fact, I used these words so many times in so many different ways that they lost any meaning. How many times could I say sorry, yet still do the same thing over and over again?

It's so easy to say "forgive me" to someone. In fact, we can use it as a bully club sometimes. One of Jesus' disciples asked Him, "How many times should I forgive my brother, seven times?" and Jesus responded, "No, multiply that by seven and you start getting the idea." Our church culture has abused this to the point that when I seek people's forgiveness I'm expecting them to simply open their arms and embrace me. If they don't instantly absolve me of my sin towards them, I become offended, the roles become reversed, and I'm now the wronged party! How has this absurdity happened? Jesus' instruction was to the person who was being asked forgiveness; He may have said "go and sin no more" to the person asking forgiveness! So we stop saying, "I'm sorry," and start asking, "What can I do to make it right?" The idea is that we are living different lives now, so we are going to lay down our lives for each other in love.

When we make amends to the people we have harmed we are demonstrating our sincerity and humility by acknowledging our wrongdoing; we offer to take action to make them whole. We aren't paying for our sins, as there is nothing we can do to fully justify ourselves before God and others. In our eighth and ninth steps we are trying to do what is right and love others the way that God has loved us.

Our eighth step is making a list of all persons we have harmed and becoming willing to make amends to them. Just like in the fourth column of the fourth step, we are going to put aside any wrongs people may have done to us. Here we are looking at our role, our behavior, what have we done, and how have we harmed others. If we have harmed someone who has done harm to us, the two actions don't cancel each other out. Our goal is to lay down *our* lives for others regardless of what they may have done to us. It's difficult and humbling to make amends to people who have wronged us. We typically take the attitude that we owe them nothing; they hurt us and we hurt them. But Christ didn't take this attitude. When we were still sinners, Christ died for us. There could be no other way—He had to be the bigger man. He laid His life down for us first, the grand gesture of love. If we're going to be imitators of Him, we must put aside our pride and sense of entitlement and be willing to right our wrongs.

So we make a list and put names and places down on paper. Whom have we harmed, whom do we need to make things right with? Are we willing to go to them and offer our actions to mend hurt feelings, to rectify financial harm, or to restore relationships? In our list we don't write down what we have done or why we need to make amends, we simply write names. Once the list is complete, it is advisable to go through it with the person who is taking you through the steps. He or she will provide indispensible guidance and advice on the soundness of the list.

There are several practical questions that typically arise with eighth step lists. Primary among them is "does so and so belong on the list?" When deciding whether or not we owe someone an amends, the principal questions we may ask are:

1) have I harmed this person or place; 2) is there a chance of redeeming a bad situation or relationship by making amends; 3) have I inhibited my ability to be of any help to this person or place because there is distrust or anger between us; and 4) is it the right thing to do? These questions are intended to lead us to a place where we are sensitive to the conscience God has given us. This is where our willingness comes in. In this step we become willing to make amends to others and to be honest about how we have harmed them; we are sensitive to God's Spirit in our hearts, actively listening and responding to His correction and guidance.

When our list is complete we review it with our sponsor and develop a plan for our ninth step. The ninth step asks us to make direct amends to the people we have harmed, except when to do so would injure them or others. We will visit our neighbors, friends, family, and colleagues in person, when possible; admit to them that we wronged them; and ask if we can do anything to make the situation right. Our goal is to make ourselves useful to God by tearing down the walls of hurt, anger and distrust that we have built up between ourselves and our fellow man. We are not asking for anyone's pity or magnanimity. We have engaged in a deeper relationship with God and are making amends in a spirit of love and humility rather than shame; therefore, we don't cower before these people or places. We are humble, not pathetic.

It is important to remember we are there to right our wrongs, not to evangelize. People are very perceptive to ulterior motives. There is no need to verbally present the gospel message to the people we have wronged, not now. In fact, we should take a moment to remember why we are there. We're there to make an amends because we have harmed these people. How do we think our message of God's forgiveness and love will be received by them at that particular time? Our actions will speak much louder than our words. If they are interested in your motives, they will ask and you will have the opportunity to share, in a tactful and appropriate way, why.

There may be many amends that require extra sensitivity, particularly regarding sexual relations. We are always considering the welfare of others and must use this as our guide in this step. If there have been affairs or improprieties that we need to make right, we are wise to consider the ramifications on people who are unaware of them. For instance, in our sex inventory we may have admitted to having an affair or improper relationship with someone in the past. You may have decided that because of it you have hurt your current spouse or significant other even if he or she were never aware of it. It is important to ask whether it would cause more harm than good to divulge this information now. There is no set rule in these delicate situations; it may be smarter to make a living amends. There may be other amends that would cause compounding harm to your family and loved ones if made; again, this is something that must be prayerfully considered with your sponsor.

Often times our actions have caused irreparable harm and certain people refuse to meet with us personally. It is understandable. We cannot force ourselves on such individuals and cause greater grief. In such cases a letter may be the best course of action. Emails and text messages don't qualify—this is a serious matter that requires a more traditional and thoughtful medium. In our letter we acknowledge our guilt and express our sincere willingness to be there if they need us or ask us to do something for them.

These particular cases are not an excuse to back down from necessary amends. Our own feelings and bank accounts are not taken into consideration when deciding whether further harm would be done. We are going to lay down our own lives for others emotionally, financially and spiritually. I have had the privilege of working on the ninth step with numerous people who had to admit to serious harm with the potential for substantial repercussions. They were willing to go to any lengths to get closer to God and they walked through the fear and stress hand in hand with God. The results have always been positive, but most of us don't know that before we make the amends. God will provide the needed strength and support if we rely on Him.

As you can see there are all types of ways to make amends. Perhaps the most important and difficult way is to make a living amends. There are people whom we love and share our lives with who wouldn't feel comfortable asking us to set things right by taking certain action. Amends to our family and loved ones require a lifelong commitment to be the child, sibling or spouse that God would have us be. Certainly we can give them the opportunity to express their discontent at our behavior, but we don't let ourselves off the hook because they've been able to vent. By living the amends we have the opportunity to demonstrate to our loved ones the power God has so graciously given us. We serve them and love them out of sincerity, not guilt or shame. Living amends, however, don't require us to be under the heel of our family and spouses. Doing so may cause them more harm than anything we have done in the past. When we let God's Spirit have perfect sway in our lives we can act appropriately and genuinely. There may be times and situations that call for us to act in stern and tough ways. Don't feel guilty about having to do this. God does it with us all the time. God disciplines those He loves. If need be we can do the same, but we can never act from a place of resentment or fear. If we are actively pursuing God and submitting our lives unselfishly to Him, He will give us the guidance we need.

Overall the amends process is humbling but purifying. Through it we begin to see how our actions have affected other people. Some people will take the opportunity to tell you, in specificity, the full extent of your harm. This is a good thing. Most significantly we are demonstrating that we are living different lives now and can be trusted if they need our help or guidance. When we have finished our ninth step we are uniquely situated to be of use to God. We have mended fences, reduced hate and restored trust. We have a special opportunity to demonstrate our altered way of life and prove that our words have substance again. Ultimately we are demonstrating love and giving others hope that there are people willing to be doers of God's word.

CHAPTER 6

On the day of Pentecost Peter was transformed by the Spirit of God and became the leader of a movement that would change the course of human civilization. He preached openly in the city of Jerusalem that Jesus of Nazareth was the long-awaited Messiah and that He had risen from the dead, proving His divinity. Only weeks earlier, Peter had denied that he even knew Jesus. Through pain and hopelessness God brought new life to Peter. It happened quickly, but he was truly transformed. It may now be the same for you; it certainly was for me. Sensitive to God's Spirit and His call on our lives, we are experiencing new freedom from anger and fear. With this come great joy, peace and purpose. This is an exciting time, full of new possibilities—God has done for us what we were unable to do on our own!

But we are not perfect—we are human. We must continue to actively pursue God in this journey, for there will be setbacks and failings. Even Peter failed after Pentecost. Paul tells us in his letter to the Galatians that he had to reprimand Peter because Peter was falling back into self-seeking and fearful behavior. In an attempt to mollify Jewish Christians, Peter began to distance himself from Gentile believers. Peter didn't want to be seen associating with Gentiles because he was afraid of what others would say about him. Paul writes, "When Peter came to Antioch, I opposed him to his face, because he was clearly in the wrong." If Peter failed, then surely we will, too. The good news is that as we pursue progress with God, we allow His Spirit to sanctify our lives and actions. We will never reach perfection but we can achieve progress. We press on to take hold of that for which Christ Jesus took hold of us.

Now that we have taken steps one through nine, we have a new framework on which to apply biblical principles. In this new context we process subsequent anger, fear and sexual misconduct. More importantly, the tools we now have can be used to continually guard against selfish behavior. We use the remaining steps to progress closer to God.

The tenth step suggests that we continue to take personal inventory and promptly admit when we are wrong. Essentially, step ten is the fourth through ninth steps rolled into one. The format of tenth step inventory is identical to that of the fourth step. When we experience new anger, we write a resentment inventory, read it, and then ask God to remove it. With new sexual issues or fear, we do the same. If we have harmed anyone we quickly make amends. Someone who has truly been changed by God through this process will continually use it.

I've had the opportunity to work through the steps with many people. I can tell you, without hesitation, that those who don't continue to write tenth step inventory and make prompt amends fail to progress spiritually and nullify the experience of the earlier steps. For alcoholics and addicts this means relapse and, potentially, death. For others it means reverting back to old habits and hopelessness. I'm reluctant to use the following analogy because it seems trite, but it works nonetheless. The first nine steps may be likened to a diet. Diets work—they do. If you practice a diet you will lose weight, feel better and get healthier. But if you reach your target weight and then go back to your old eating and exercise patterns, you will put the weight back on and be right back where you began. The same is true with the steps. If you have had a life-changing experience and learned a new way to connect with God, you must continue in it or else you will be back where you began.

The tenth step also provides a way to develop deep and genuine relationships with other people in the process. You will likely have a select group of people, maybe only one or two, whom you regularly read inventory to. These people will know you on a level that few others do. They will be able to hold you accountable, give you proper guidance, and support you; you will be able to do the same for them. To know and be known is perhaps one of the greatest human desires. Tenth step inventory gives us the chance to be transparent with others and establish lasting relationships built on honesty. Reading inventory is humbling. The best friendships we can have are those where we can be humble, where there is no need to impress or to maintain a façade. These friends know who we really are and still love us. This is something that I hope each and every one of you will be able to experience.

Typically inventory should be read privately with one other person without any comments, but perhaps some of you will be bold enough to start a weekly group with others who have taken steps. During these gatherings you may have the opportunity to read inventory to the group. This is not a bad idea, so long as we remain mindful of the confidential nature of inventory. There must be demonstrated commitment and trust among everyone present. Also, the person reading inventory should be careful not to use tenth step inventory as a way to vent or gain selfish attention. Remember, inventory is confession to God in the presence of another; it is not a means for receiving pity or occupying the spotlight. Those who hear inventory should not comment on it unless asked to by the person reading it. If so, comments should be limited to how the person could be more honest in the fourth column. Inventory is a powerful tool that can reach deep into ourselves; if you really need someone to comment on your inventory, select a person who has demonstrated practice with and understanding of the step process.

Concurrent with the tenth step is the eleventh, which suggests that we seek to improve, through prayer and meditation, our contact with God. This may seem obvious, but the challenge of the eleventh step lies in how we pray and meditate. Through this process we have identified our selfishness and asked God to remove it. Now our prayers must reflect that by centering on others. We ask God to provide for our needs so that we can be of maximum use to our neighbors. Recall James' words: you ask but do not receive because you ask with wrong motives, so that you can spend it on your pleasures. So we ask God to give us our daily bread; to help us seek His kingdom and His will first; and to bless others, especially our enemies, through us. God knows what we need and He will provide it, if we seek His kingdom first, if we act in love toward others, if we constantly lay our lives down for our friends and neighbors, and if we are willing to do what He asks us.

It is also particularly important that we pray for others when we promise them we will. If we tell someone that we will pray for them, we do it. It would be better to hold our tongue and not promise to pray, rather than say we will and don't. We are people of action. Our word has become our bond. Furthermore, we will quickly learn that when we promise to pray for others and actually do it, our care and consideration for them will increase, as we become more sensitive to their needs and feelings.

There are several instances in the gospels where we are told that Jesus withdrew to a solitary place to pray, often in the morning before His disciples got up. This should be an example to us. Each and every morning we should find time to pray, alone, with God. We ask Him to guide our day and make us attentive to the needs of others.

We also meditate on how we can serve Him better. Take time to be quiet and still before the busyness of the day begins. His peace and direction will be our guide and strengthen us if we learn the discipline of silence. If you find that you are confused or have taken your will back, you should find a quiet place to be silent and still, physically and mentally, so that you can be receptive to what God would have you do. If you are meeting with others who have taken steps, before you begin your gathering collectively take two or three minutes of silent meditation. A few minutes of purposeful stillness will help guide your prayer and conversation, and it will help you realign with God and be present for the people who need you.

My hope for each of you is that you will learn and practice the discipline of selfless prayer and silent meditation. Our job isn't to convince God to give us the things we need, for He will. We must learn to recognize His still small voice and, at times, be still and peaceful even in the midst of the tempests of life. God will bring this if we allow Him to.

CHAPTER 7

It was a brisk spring day and a few of the people who had brought me through the steps met me at a charitable golf tournament to play in my grouping. The sun was shining, the snow was gone and the grass was green. The long winter had faded away and the newness of the spring brought that feeling only a New Englander can fully appreciate. It was going to be a great day, a time to relax and catch up with some friends.

I felt as if my life was beginning a new season, too. I was four months sober and emerging from a cold, harsh time that had brought me to the brink of destruction. I had no clue what to do with the rest of my life; I wasn't going back to California or my legal career. That door was shut. An old high school friend was kind enough to hire me as a painter for his company even though I was completely inept at professional painting. My future was wide open but uncertain. So my friends and I teed off at the first hole, ready to begin a great round—even though I was inept at golf, too.

While on the fourteenth or fifteenth hole, almost ready to finish our game, I recalled a conversation I had with someone a few days earlier. This person had mentioned to me that he owned a house that would be perfect for a group home, maybe even a recovery home for alcoholics and addicts. He was trying to sell it and asked if I knew of anyone who would be interested in buying it. Almost as an after-thought, I mentioned it to my friends as I took another hacking swing somewhere deep in the rough. Their response to me was surprising. "You should do it," they said. Me? No. What did I know about running a sober living community? I was only months sober—how was I qualified to teach and guide others in the step process, when I was still a babe in this new life? But they urged me to pursue the opportunity with the help of someone in the area who had wanted to start a recovery home for some time. They assured me that it wasn't the length of my sobriety that mattered, it was the quality. By the time we finished the tournament they had convinced me to at least investigate the possibility. So I did. Seven months later we opened the doors to a new sober living community based on the 12 steps as they are laid out in the book *Alcoholics Anonymous*.

Without me even looking, God had brought new purpose and direction to my life. He gave us the opportunity and the privilege help others develop a conscious contact with God so that they could recover in the same way we had. He also brought a lifelong friend and brother to work alongside me to accomplish it. There were, and still are, tremendous trials and struggles to build and maintain the community, but, at least as I write this, God is allowing it to continue as a place of hope and healing for many. God gave me the undeserved honor of making my twelfth step work a calling.

But what about you? How will you work your twelfth step? As I wrote earlier, the way the steps are laid out here are not for the alcoholic or addict. There are particular issues that the A/A faces that are not dealt with in this particular step application. I believe it may be counter-productive for the A/A to replace the original 12 steps with the steps as they are laid out here. Please don't try it. If you know of someone who may be an A/A, the best course of action is to refer them to another A/A who has recovered by taking steps as laid out in the book *Alcoholics Anonymous*. If you can, find someone who has developed a conscious contact with God through the steps, not simply through meeting attendance.

Perhaps it is at this step that we differ most substantially from the original 12 step model. Our twelfth step suggests that we practice these principles in all our affairs, and carry this message to others who need it. But who "needs it" and how do we "practice these principles in all our affairs"?

Maybe the best way to begin answering the first question is to ask ourselves what we have gained through the process. Take some time to reflect and meditate on what God has done for you, what new freedom and hope you have gained from taking steps. Have you been released from self-pity and apathy? Are you more aware of your selfishness and hypocrisy? Think about how your actions are different. Is your faith having demonstrable results through your works? Have your relationships with your family and friends begun to change? Are you more considerate of the needs of others? Do you have a new sense that God is real? Do you now believe, deep in your soul, that He has the power to bring healing and restoration? Do you read the teachings of Jesus with a greater understanding of its relevance to your daily life? Are you a doer of the word and not just a hearer? Are you using inventory as a way to deal with resentment and fear, asking God to remove them with His power?

Once we have experienced these things ourselves we become keenly aware that many others need the same experience. Our churches are filled to the brim with people who desire a deeper and more personal connection with God. We were those people! We have found a method to express our faith and a context to express our love and trust in God. There are many who need a practical program to help them apply the Bible and incorporate it into their lives. They are all around us: sitting in our churches, attending our small groups, working beside us in our ministries, and even living in our homes.

This is not, however, an indictment on most church leadership; this is an indictment on us. Most Christian communities are led by long-suffering pastors. I know—I really do. Today's pastors are asked to perform the duties of CEO, counselor, teacher, visionary, development officer, chief of staff, landscaper, handyman, community liaison, activity coordinator, and so on. We have failed them as members and parishioners. It is time for us to give back to them, to support their work and lives. We need to be sensitive to their sacrifice, so we start by telling them about our experience with the process and expressing our willingness to help others who they think might benefit from it. Be mindful not to act as crusaders for this course. The steps haven't changed us—God has. There is no magic or inherent power in the step process; it is just one tool to help us connect with God. It's a reformatting of Biblical principles, not a reformulation. If your life has genuinely changed, your pastor will see it and ask you to help others in the same way you have been helped.

There are also people who will simply notice that we look and act differently. They'll ask us what has happened and we can tell them of our rigorous process of self-reflection and recommitment to God. If they want what we have, we can offer to take them through the steps. If they balk at the idea of taking the 12 steps, that's ok. They may not need to. We can help them by being a true friend who can speak truth and love into their lives. We can love them as God has loved us. The primary message emerging from this process is that we lay down our lives for our friends and neighbors. We can certainly do that without forcing them into taking steps. God may have a different path for them. But, if they are eager to do what we have done, don't hesitate to take time out of your schedule to work with them. This may be the very tool they need.

Some of us may also start a weekly or monthly gathering in our Christian community of people who have taken these steps. If this is the case you can, with great care and consideration, invite those you think may be interested. You do not want those whom you invited to feel you are identifying them as dysfunctional or maladjusted; if they think this then walls of defensiveness and anger may build up in them. You should assure them that this is something you think they may be interested in, but if they're not, it's alright. Remember, we needed this because we weren't responding to the gospel message the way we should have been. This is not true of everyone. We take our own inventory, not other's.

However we may find people who "need it," it is important that when we first meet with them we listen. We are quick to listen and slow to speak. Why do they feel they need a new and practical way to apply Jesus' teachings to their lives? What are they struggling with, and what has been their test of faith? They may be questioning the truth of the Bible, the authenticity of the Christian faith, even the existence of God. It's okay. We are not there to judge their current state, but to help them out of it. We resist the temptation to provide quick and canned answers. We listen and empathize with them; then we can share our story. Honestly and openly tell them where you have been, what your life and relationship with God looked like, and what your struggles and failures were. Be transparent. Tell them what God has done for you, what you did, and how God has changed you. You have the chance to give hope that God can do for them what He has done for you. Most importantly, though, they need to be able to identify with you and trust that you understand where they are coming from. If you know of someone else in your group that could be of greater assistance to them, you can put them in contact with each other. Please don't be disappointed that you yourself can't take them through the process. God has used you in a wonderful way. If you have been able to put people together who can help one another, it is a great privilege to be a part of that. All in all, we aren't out to create an exclusive group of people; we don't hoard the step process or make it difficult for others to do the same if they are willing and eager.

Finally, the steps, as they are laid out here are not an instrument of verbal evangelization, but a tool to help our lives demonstrate that we are disciples of Jesus. Our lives are living testimonies to the grace and power of God. By practicing the steps in all our affairs, we allow the Holy Spirit to use us more effectively to reach others with the good news.

Faith, hope, commitment, confession, atonement, and perseverance are the legacy of this process through the power of God. May they be yours. May you find the peace and love of God as you go forth to bless others and live with renewed purpose and determination, and may all our lives be a light in a dark and needy world.

APPENDIX – MIND/ BODY DISEASE MODEL

Alcoholics and addicts who are working through the classic and traditional 12 steps of recovery will be introduced to the mind/body disease model during their first step. It is difficult to directly apply this to individuals who are taking steps simply as a means of spiritual formation or expansion. However, for those who are interested, I will briefly explain it. Some addictions that are not mind-altering substance-based may generate a similar phenomenon as the model I will describe. In particular, sex and food addictions may produce certain chemical and hormonal changes that could possibly develop into this type of disease. If you find that you can identify, in particularity and totality, with this disease model and come to believe that you are struggling with an addiction it is advisable for you to take steps within a formal step-based recovery program. For those not struggling with a chronic addiction you may still be able to admit that certain sins have unique power over you. In such situations you may find it easier to take a first step if you recognize that your powerlessness is comparable to an addict or alcoholic.

Alcoholism and addiction are spiritual illnesses manifested in the mind and body. That is why I don't believe anyone is born an alcoholic or addict. People can have personality traits or physiological characteristics that make it easier to develop addictive behaviors, but alcoholism and addiction are illnesses that are developed over repeated and prolonged abuse of alcohol and drugs. The illness is characterized by an inability to stop using or "stay stopped." That is, when the disease is fully generated, alcoholics or addicts (the "A/A") cannot stop using in and of themselves and, if through some means outside of themselves they are forced to stop, they cannot stay abstinent permanently.

When an A/A is without drugs or alcohol they are consumed with the desire to drink or use. If they cannot they are filled with restlessness, irritability and discontentedness ("RID"). No activity, work, pleasure or pain is sufficient to distract them enough to break their incessant desire to drink or use, because only drinking or using will bring them mental relief from the RID they constantly experience. Their mind is broken; they have developed a mental obsession for drugs or alcohol. No amount of consequence or motivation is sufficient to relieve the mental obsession. They have chosen to use drugs or alcohol to relieve themselves from the stress, boredom and pain of life for so long, with such intensity, that they don't know how to handle life without it. Alcohol and drugs become the primary means of coping with reality for the A/A. Using makes them feel good at first, but because of the physical effects of it, over time, they are forced to use merely to get a sense of normalcy. Life becomes intolerable without alcohol or drugs. When the disease has reached its final stages the A/A cannot imagine life with or without substances. They become suicidal or totally consumed with anxiety and depression.

Physically, the A/A has developed an allergy as described in Alcoholics Anonymous literature. One drink or dose of drugs causes them to desire more and more of it until they have passed out or run out of money. This is the physical craving. The average person would be able to stop when he or she felt sick or out of control, but the A/A cannot stop; their body craves more of the substance.

The mental obsession can be cured through actively working the 12 steps as laid out in the book *Alcoholics Anonymous*. This is what the text of the book keeps referring to when it uses the word "recovered"; the A/A has recovered from the mental obsession. But the physical craving cannot be cured. An A/A can never drink or use in safety again. They will always have the allergy. It is akin to people who have a peanut allergy. They don't have to worry about getting sick from peanuts if they never eat them, but if they do eat them they may die.

When new A/As are taken through the first step, the person taking them through it will weave in personal examples of how he or she experienced the mental obsession and physical craving. If the new A/A truly has the disease and is honest about it, they will identify with the person and become open to a solution. This is why alcoholics and addicts are uniquely situated to help other A/As. They can identify with the mental obsession and physical craving in a way that non-A/As can't.

1284265R00044

Made in the USA
San Bernardino, CA
07 December 2012